The Spiritual Journey of the Stations of the Cross

An everyday devotional of the journey of Jesus Christ

Written by Daniel L. Grant

Illustrated by Arlene RB Sullivan

iUniverse, Inc.

New York   Bloomington

Scriptural quotes taken from the King James Bible

iUniverse books may be ordered through booksellers or by contacting:

iUniverse
1663 Liberty Drive
Bloomington, IN 47403
www.iuniverse.com
1-800-Authors (1-800-288-4677)

ISBN: 978-1-4401-8770-4 (sc)
ISBN: 978-1-4401-8771-1 (ebook)

Printed in the United States of America

iUniverse rev. date: 02/23/2010

Foreword

The second Vatican council in the constitution on the sacred liturgy (art. 13) directs that popular devotions be derived from sacred liturgy. This devotional workbook incorporates a scriptural basis for eight of the Stations of the Cross and a traditional basis for five of the Stations.

While attempting to provide a scriptural and traditional basis for the Stations of the Cross, the medium of art and the written word permits us to relive the drama of the timeless events of the Passion of Jesus Christ, Our Lord.

May you be inspired by this journey with Christ to live your faith with your brothers and sisters in Christ.

Fr. Carmen Buono

Introduction

The Spiritual Journey of the Stations of the Cross.

For God so loved the world,

that he gave his only begotten Son,

That whosoever believeth in him

should not perish but

have ever lasting life.

John 3:16

It has been called the "Via Dolorosa" the "Via Crucis", the "Way of Sorrows" or just the "Way". The Stations of the Cross represent the last hours of the journey of Christ to the Cross and the promise of everlasting life for Christians. It is meant to symbolize the last hours and the suffering and ultimate punishment that the Son of God had to endure to bring everlasting life to the faithful. It is meant to physically transport the believer to the actual trial, punishment and the steps taken by Jesus Christ, not by the written word but by the act of stopping at each of the Stations and contemplating what happened to him at that spot and at that very moment. Thereby adding yourself to the suffering and ultimate salvation that Jesus brought to all who will have faith and believe.

The tradition was established by Franciscan Monks in the 1400's to help believers make a spiritual journey and meditate as they make this most inspiring pilgrimage. It focuses on the chief scenes of Christ's last hours and the suffering he endured to bring all who follow him to an everlasting and eternal life "in his Father's House". Originally the building of the Fourteen Stations had to be overseen by the Franciscan Order to insure that it was blessed by the Church. St. Francis had gone to Jerusalem himself and walked in the actual steps of our Savior and had established what is believed to be the first live Nativity scene while he was there. He also knew that millions of the faithful would never get the opportunity to walk in the actual steps of Jesus of Nazareth.

Each Station which has remained a constant and extremely moving devotion for Roman Catholics and other Christians, since it was begun, is based on either scriptural or traditional facts surrounding the last hours of Jesus Christ. Each Station is meant to have a meditation and prayer for the pilgrim. It is in fact a journey of devotion not simply a reading of scripture or a stationary prayer. It is supposed to allow the pilgrim to share and add their own suffering to the suffering of Jesus Christ. In doing so the faithful are invited by Christ to his Father's House and it can be a faith-lifting and faith-building experience.

Stations of the Cross Traditional or Scriptural

The original Stations of the Cross were based on both a scriptural and a traditional balance and not every Station reflects a passage in the New Testament and is supported with a scriptural reference. Only Stations One, Two, Five, Eight, Ten, Eleven, Twelve, Thirteen and Fourteen are found to have a clear scriptural basis. Stations Three, Four, Six, Seven, and Nine are not referenced in Scripture. They are based on the traditional beliefs of what had occurred at each Station but for purposes of meditation and devotion they are just as valid. Tradition should have no less value on your journey of devotion. Tradition can be the inspired word of God to the person who established the Tradition. The benefit is derived by the journey and contemplation and prayer that you feel and say as you move from Station to Station.

In 1991, Pope John Paul II introduced new Stations so that each would have a scriptural basis. These are called the Scriptural Way of the Cross. Every Station has a reference to Scripture. He established these Stations in the Coliseum in Rome, where he would observe the Stations and walk to each on Good Friday each year. He would lead a procession of the Faithful until he was no longer able to physically do it and then a stage was set up for him so that he could be witness to the journeys of others.

In 2007, Pope Benedict XVI approved this set of Stations for meditation and devotion for use by the public. We have included both sets of the Stations in order to provide the most faith lifting experience for all.

Although originally developed as a Roman Catholic devotion it is no less meaningful to all who call themselves Christians. The suffering Jesus Christ endured, the ridicule and pain he experienced and the sacrifice for all that would be saved, are the very essence of the Stations of the Cross. It is a pilgrimage that all those faithful in Jesus Christ would benefit from. The experience of meditating on each and every Station as one follows the events of the day literally by walking to each Station can be far more meaningful and devotional then even an hour in church. Although the time that most Christians devote themselves to the Stations of the Cross is traditionally Good Friday, the act of symbolically walking the last hours with Jesus Christ has a tremendous spiritual effect anytime it is done.

Each Station starts with a universal prayer and the scriptural reference when appropriate. We include meditations and a brief description of the Station from either Scripture or tradition. Each Pilgrim is encouraged to meditate on the subject of that particular Station. Join yourself to the suffering of Jesus Christ to help understand why it was that he had to suffer so and meditate on the fact that he did this for the eternal life of the faithful.

With that let us begin our journey.

The Fourteen Stations of the Cross

Traditional Version

Station I   Jesus is Condemned to Death

We adore you, O Lord Jesus Christ and we bless you.

Because by your Holy Cross, You have redeemed the world.

Matthew 27: 1-2.

1. When the morning was come, all the chief priests and elders of the people took counsel against Jesus to put him to death.

2. And when they had bound him, they led him away and delivered him to Pontius Pilate the Governor.

Matthew 27: 20-23.

20. But the chief priests and elders persuaded the multitude that they should ask for Barabbas and destroy Jesus.

21. The Governor answered and said unto them, Whether the twain will ye that I release unto you? They said Barabbas.

22. Pilate saith unto them, What shall I do then with Jesus which is called the Christ? They all say unto him, Let him be Crucified.

23. And the Governor said, Why, What evil hath he done? But they cried out the more, saying, let him be crucified.

Meditation:

Consider that Jesus has now been arrested, bound and accused of blasphemy, the priests and elders here have brought Jesus to Pontius Pilate, the Roman Governor of Judea, because only he has the power to condemn Jesus to death. Pilate finds no fault with Jesus under Roman Law but the priests and elders demand that he be crucified. Pilate gives them a choice in front of the gathered crowd to either free a criminal named Barabbas or to free Jesus of Nazareth but they incite the crowd to say free Barabbas and Pilate orders Jesus to be beaten and washing his hands of it, Jesus is taken to be crucified.

Your meditation:

_____
_____
_____
_____
_____
_____
_____
_____
_____

Station I

Station II   Jesus is Given His Cross

We adore You O Lord Jesus Christ, and we bless you.

Because of Your Holy Cross, You have redeemed the world.

John 19:16-17

16. They delivered him therefore unto them to be crucified   And they took Jesus and led him away

17. And he bearing his cross went forth into a place called the place of the skull, which is called in the Hebrew, Golgotha.

Meditation:

At that time only Romans could conduct an execution and in the practice of crucifixion, the accused would carry their own cross to the place of death. This was the burden that Jesus had to carry. While this was done as a punishment, Jesus did it out of promise and eternal love. It was part of the redemption of man that he carry this burden and while suffering the beating and crown of thorns and the humiliation that he had undergone that day this physical burden he also had to endure. His burden was so great yet his promise so much greater still for in that promise lay the everlasting life of the faithful. This cross he did bear for all mankind. We can but reflect in wonder at his sacrifice.

Your meditation:

Station II

Station III **Jesus Falls for the First Time**

We adore You, O Lord Jesus Christ and we bless you.

Because by Your Holy Cross, You have redeemed the world.

Jesus stumbles and falls to the ground under the weight of the cross while the guards beat him to get him back on his feet. His execution awaits. He struggles to regain his footing and to begin again, the journey to the fulfillment of God's promise. His physical form cannot move forward. The Cross which is built to hold a man is made of rough hewn wood, heavy to bear. Tall enough to crucify a man, the base drags on the ground and the crossbeam digs into his shoulder.

Meditation:

We all have a cross to bear and by joining our crosses to his we can join in the triumph of overcoming our personal crosses. How much greater was his cross and then how much greater is the blessing he brought to us by carrying his burdens to the final redemption. Picture the rough stone and dirt path he had to walk while trying to carry that heavy rough hewn cross. Picture the crowds ridiculing him as he walked alone with his burden. He falls. Consider our own obstacles that cause us to stumble as we carry the burdens of our own life. Do we not falter ourselves without having the additional burden of the weight of all the sins of mankind on our back? Where are the throngs who made his entry to Jerusalem such a triumph? Where are the disciples who made the journey of the last three years with him now? Those who witnessed his teachings and the occurrence of the miracles have now also abandoned him. Does this not happen in our own lives? Do we not also feel abandoned at times of need? The solitary journey of Christ is a painful but necessary one for the fulfillment of the promise he made to us. Stand now before his struggle and stand with him.

Your meditation:

_____

_____

_____

_____

_____

_____

_____

_____

_____

_____

_____

_____

_____

_____

_____

_____

_____

_____

Station III

Station IV   **Jesus Meets his Mother**

We adore You O Lord Jesus Christ, and we bless you

Because by your Holy Cross, you have redeemed the world.

Meditation:

It is hard to imagine any mother seeing the child she bore being punished so and knowing that the real suffering had yet to begin. Mary was in the crowd watching as her son was beaten. Watching as her son was taunted and reviled by the crowd. Flesh of her flesh brought into this world to come to this very moment and yet still as a mother who loved her son, she suffered with him. Mary fought to get through the crowd to position herself where she would be able to come face to face with him. She so wanted him to know that he was not alone. That he know that she was with him on this last short and suffering journey to his death. She was desperate to bring him what comfort she could if she could only get through the crowd to have him set eyes on her. Finally she found a doorway that he would have to pass and she fought against the crowd until at last he was within sight of her. Their eyes met and he was comforted by her sight as she was comforted by having their eyes meet.

When our loved ones suffer will we not do everything in our power to bring what relief we can to them? Will we all not yearn to share in their suffering, to feel their pain and by sharing it do we not help to bring comfort? Mary knew the journey that was the prophecy that Jesus had to fulfill but in that hour she would have done anything she could have to take that burden from him. It was for these last hours that the Angel of the Lord had visited her so long ago and it is for this hour that she had been blessed to give birth to God's redemption of the world.

Your meditation:

_____

_____

_____

_____

_____

_____

_____

_____

_____

_____

_____

_____

_____

_____

_____

_____

_____

_____

Station V   Simone of Cyrene Carries the Cross

We adore you O Lord Jesus Christ, and we bless you.

Because by your Holy Cross, You have redeemed the world.

Matthew 27:32. And as they came out, they found a man named Simon by name and they compelled him to carry the cross.

Mark 15:21.   And they compel one Simon, a Cyrenian, who passed by, coming out of the country, the father of Alexander and Rufus to bear his cross.

Luke 23:26.   And as they led him away, they lay hold upon one Simon, a Cyrenian, coming out of the country, and on him they laid the cross, that he might bear it after Jesus.

Meditation:

It was Passover and all Jerusalem was filled with Israelites from far and wide, come to celebrate the Passover. They had come to worship and bring their sacrifices to the temple. They came from all over Judea and while many had heard of the promise of Jesus many had not seen or heard him speak the word of God.

There is no indication from scripture that Simon was a follower of Jesus Christ only that he was selected from the multitude for the holiest of duties. He helped Christ in a way that any Christian would have been moved to do. He eased the burden of the cross from our Savior's shoulders. He eased the pain of the Cross from digging into the flesh of our Lord. Which of us would not give up our lives to have been that person? Here at this station we can meditate on how we would serve to lighten the load of Jesus and how we can serve others as he has served us.

Jesus often taught of the importance of how we treat each other. In fact it is central to his teachings that we love each other as we love God. He had preached that we must relieve suffering and serve each other. That whosoever would be the last will be first.

Your meditation:

_____
_____
_____
_____
_____
_____
_____
_____
_____
_____
_____
_____
_____
_____
_____
_____

Station VI   **Veronica Wipes the Face of Jesus**

We adore You, O Lord Jesus Christ, and we bless you.

Because by Your Holy Cross, You have redeemed the world.

Meditation:

Here at station VI we celebrate Veronica. Many of those in the crowd reviled Jesus but many also wailed and wept for his suffering. Many of the women sought to comfort him as he struggled with the Cross. He had fallen under the weight of it. He had been scourged and mocked. The Soldiers had put a crown of thorns on his head which dug into his flesh causing him to have blood dripping down his face and into his eyes, making it all the more difficult for him to see the rough hewn streets as he walked.

The Soldiers beat back the crowds, those who wanted to comfort and those who wanted to scorn in equal measure. They used harsh methods to keep the crowds back from Jesus often swinging clubs and lashing out at will at mourner and mocker alike.

Veronica was not intimidated by the force the soldiers used but went through the crowds and came to Jesus and gently wiped the blood and sweat from his face with her veil. When she was at last forced away she beheld the image of Jesus on her veil and was amazed. What would you have done? Would you have the strength to have done what Veronica had done? Here we can see the devotion of Veronica, risking much to bring comfort to our Lord. Many would not. The soldiers were known for their brutality toward men and women alike. Jesus repaid her with the image of his likeness on her veil as a testament to her devotion to him. In the hour of his greatest suffering he rewarded her for her kindness. Do we do that? Are we aware of the risks and effort people take on behalf of helping or being kind to us?

Your meditation:

_____

_____

_____

_____

_____

_____

_____

_____

_____

_____

_____

_____

_____

_____

_____

_____

_____

_____

_____

Station VI

Station VII   **Jesus Falls the Second Time**

We adore You, O Lord Jesus Christ, and we bless you.

Because by Your Holy Cross, You have redeemed the World.

Meditation:

Jesus is weary beyond belief. He falls again for a second time on the rough road of stone and dirt. The crowd presses in on him and the cross is too heavy to bear. Simon takes the weight of the cross and Jesus gets to his feet again and continues his journey.

    We fall. We do it many times over and over again. We fall to temptation, we fall in our responsibility, we fall in our devotion to being one of the faithful. We need to be as Jesus was and rise again and renew our faith. Jesus rose for us in order to complete his mission of redemption for the world. We need to do it as well for our own redemption. Jesus rose so that we may rise. Jesus set the example of an abiding faith that we can and should follow. Many times we let him down but he has shown us the way and by his example we can follow though we fall many times. Jesus faced the ridicule and distain of the crowd and got back up anyway. He faced the humiliation of his punishment with a glad heart knowing that his sacrifice will lead to the salvation of the many and an everlasting life in his Father's house. All we need do is to recognize that sacrifice and rise ourselves when we fall and don't want go on.

Surely he has born our griefs and carried our sorrows: yet we did esteem him stricken, smitten of God and afflicted.

But he was wounded for our transgressions; he was bruised for our iniquities: the chastisement of our peace was upon him and with our stripes we are healed.

Isaiah 56:4-5

Your meditation:

_____
_____
_____
_____
_____
_____
_____
_____
_____
_____
_____
_____
_____
_____
_____

Station VII

Station VIII   Jesus Meets the Daughters of Jerusalem

We adore You, O Lord Jesus Christ, and we bless you.

Because by Your Holy Cross, You have redeemed the world.

Luke 23:27-29.

27. And there followed a great company of people, and of women, which also bewailed and lamented him.

28. But Jesus turning unto them said, "Daughters of Jerusalem, weep not for me, but weep for yourselves, and for your children.

29. For Behold the days are coming, in which they shall say, "blessed are the barren and the wombs that never bare"

Meditation:

Jesus continues to struggle with the cross and out of the gathered crowd of people who are reviling him comes righteous women who are weeping for him. They seek to comfort him but Jesus tells them of a coming tribulation coming for those who do not follow the Lord their God. Generations yet unborn will bear the sins of this day and living a righteous life will reward them. He wants them to understand that a price will be paid for those that are not the faithful. We should feel the burden he has undertaken to save us and bring everlasting life to us but also to understand that everlasting life is not without a price, He pays the price for us and all we have to do is follow him and follow God's Law. Those who will not will pay a price hard to bear and suffer because of it. His sacrifice has sealed the promise but we still must understand that sacrifice and live our lives as if it is a sacrifice that we shared.

Your meditation:

_____
_____
_____
_____
_____
_____
_____
_____
_____
_____
_____
_____
_____
_____
_____
_____
_____
_____

Station VIII

Station IX　　　　　　**Jesus Falls the Third Time**

We adore You, O Lord Jesus Christ and we bless you.

Because by your Holy Cross, You have redeemed the world.

Meditation:

The Way is nearing the end. The journey is almost complete. Jesus falls for the third time in this terrible journey. He lies prone in the dust from which man has come. Wracked with pain and covered with blood and dirt, he lies as the subject of derision and ridicule. Some in the crowd mock his suffering. The Priests who condemned him point to him on the ground with distain. How could this be the Messiah who was promised? How could this condemned man be anything more than a pretender? See how he suffers so. Would not the Son of God come in glory and strength?

We know from the scriptures that Jesus was born fully man and fully God. The man lying in the dust of the street now suffers as any man would who was punished so. It is what makes the promise so real for all of us. That he can suffer and pay a sacrifice so terrible is what makes the promise he makes to us so real. We reflect on this suffering as a real atonement for our sins and Jesus has taken the burden of those sins unto himself. He suffers so we can go to his Father's house free of the sins of the world.

We near the end of our journey but the end is not without pain.

Your meditation:

_____
_____
_____
_____
_____
_____
_____
_____
_____
_____
_____
_____
_____
_____
_____
_____
_____
_____
_____
_____

Station IX

Station X   **Jesus is Stripped of his Garments**

We adore You, O Lord Jesus Christ, and we Bless You.

Because by Your Holy Cross, You have redeemed the world.

Luke 23:34.

Then Jesus said, Father forgive them for they know what not they do and they parted his raiment and cast lots.

Psalms 22:18

They part my garments among them and cast lots upon my vesture.

Meditation:

They have arrived at the place of crucifixion and have stripped Jesus of his outer garments as was promised in Psalms and they are now ready to give him the punishment but what is the reaction of Jesus? He asks God to forgive them, forgive them all saying "Father, Forgive them for they know what not they do." He seeks no judgment on that which was promised to happen. This is the cost of redemption and those who have condemned him and those that have carried it out are simply completing the task which had been divinely ordered by our Father. The atonement must be complete as it was written. We meditate on the very source of our salvation and eternal life, paid for by this highest of all prices. It is all out of our hands and all we need do is to accept that our Savior took this journey for our redemption. Can we do no less then believe in Christ's delivering salvation to us when he took this journey for that very salvation? A child can understand when a sacrifice is made to ensure his safety. Can we not understand and believe that this sacred blood was shed on our behalf?

They took his cloths and laid him down on the Cross in a death sentence that would give us eternal life in his Father's House so that we may live forever with him. That is the promise that he gave and sealed it with his sacrifice.

Your meditation:

_____
_____
_____
_____
_____
_____
_____
_____
_____
_____
_____
_____
_____
_____
_____

Station X

Station XI   Jesus is Nailed to the Cross

We adore You, O Lord Jesus Christ, and we bless you.

Because by Your Holy Cross, You have redeemed the world.

Luke 23:33.

And when they came to the place which is called Calvary, there they crucified him, and the malefactors, one on the right hand and the other on the left.

Mark 15:25-28

25. And it was the third hour and they crucified him.

26. And the superscription of his accusation was written over,
THE KING OF THE JEWS.

27. And with him they crucify two thieves, the one on his right hand and the other on his left.

28. And the scripture was fulfilled, which saith, And he was numbered with the transgressors.

Meditation:

As we reach this spot the full knowledge of our journey is upon us. We have seen our savior suffer and be reviled and we bear witness to all that we have seen. We bring with us our devotion to his sacrifice and our devotion to his relieving us of our sins. We bring a sense of the pain that he suffered and we have shared in that pain with him. We wait now for the inevitable outcome and we watch as the crowd mocks him and can do nothing but stand silent because this is the fulfillment of the prophesy. His disciples are in the crowd but their fear makes them silent. They have been hiding in the crowd for the whole journey. He has made this way of sorrows alone but now we have walked with him. We bring our own fears and sorrows with us to share in his pain and with that we share in the redemption he has promised and that promise has been sealed with his blood.

Your meditation:

_____
_____
_____
_____
_____
_____
_____
_____
_____
_____
_____
_____
_____
_____
_____

Station XI

Station XII   **Jesus Dies on the Cross.**

We adore You, O Lord Jesus Christ, and we bless You.

Because by Your Holy Cross, You have redeemed the world.

Eloi, Eloi, Lama sabachthani?

Mark 16:34

At the ninth hour Jesus Cried with a loud voice, saying, Eloi, Eloi, lama sabachthani? Which has been interpreted, My God my God why has thou forsaken me?

John 19:30

When Jesus, therefore had received the vinegar he said it is finished and he bowed his head, and gave up the ghost.

Luke 23:46-47

46. And when Jesus had cried with a loud voice, he said, Father, into thy hands I commend my spirit: and having said thus he gave up the ghost.

47. Now when the centurion saw what was done, he glorified God, saying certainly this was a righteous man.

Meditation:

Jesus cries out from the Cross and darkness covers Jerusalem as his spirit passes. The Temple Veil is torn and silence spreads out over the multitude. Even the Roman soldiers fear for what they have done. In his final hours Jesus has given forgiveness to his persecutors. He has cried out to God in pain and suffering, seeking God's help. Let this terrible last journey be over. Each of us can feel the suffering and pain and now that the end is here we can praise God that it is finished. Jesus is beyond the reach of mankind and those who have hurt him and made him the object of so much scorn and pain. Jesus said as his spirit passed "It is Finished."

What do we the faithful do to atone for mankind's part in this. How do we show the devotion to show we understand and have suffered with Jesus as we walk this last journey with him. Jesus died in this most terrible way for our salvation. He died for our eternal life. He died to give the faithful a room in his Father's house and he has gone on to prepare it for us.

Your meditation:

_____

_____

_____

_____

_____

_____

_____

_____

Station XII

Station XIII   Jesus is Taken from the Cross

We adore You, O Lord Jesus Christ, and we bless you.

Because by Your Holy Cross, you have redeemed the world.

Luke 23:50-53.

50. And behold there was a man named Joseph, a counselor; and he was a good man and just:

51. The same had not consented to the counsel and deed of them: and he was from Arimathea, a city of Jews, who also waited for the Kingdom of God.

52. This man went to Pilate and begged the body of Jesus.

53. And he took it down and wrapped it in linen.

Mark 15:44-46.

44. And Pilate marveled if he were already dead and calling unto him a centurion he asked him if he were a while dead.

45. And when he knew it of the centurion he gave the body to Joseph.

46. And he bought fine linen and took him down and wrapped him in the linen.

Meditation:

We understand now that the people who so lovingly took the body of Jesus Christ down from the terrible Cross knew nothing of what was to occur in the following days. Their love was based on his teachings and the promise of salvation that he gave them. They revered him for who he was and who they believed him to be. Now we know the Kingdom of God and that is what they could only have had faith in. The believed what he had foretold but knew not how it would come about. We see clearly while they could only see dimly and theirs is an example of the faith that we all should have in order to gain the Kingdom of God.

Joseph risked much to claim the body of Jesus by going to Pilate. It could not be hidden from those who had mocked Jesus and asked for his execution but he went ahead and did it anyway. His body needed to be prepared in the manner of the custom and his followers who had been so afraid before now came forward to do what had to be done to prepare Jesus for burial.

Your meditation:

_____

_____

_____

_____

_____

_____

_____

_____

Station XIV   Jesus is Laid in the Tomb

We adore You, O Lord Jesus Christ, and we bless you.

Because by your Holy Cross, You have redeemed the world.

Mark 15:46-47

46. And he laid him in a sepulcher which was hewn out of a rock and rolled a stone unto the door of it.

47. And Mary Magdalene and Mary the mother of Jesus beheld where he was laid.

Matthew 28:60-61

60. And laid it in his own new tomb which he had hewn out of rock and he rolled a great stone to the door of the sepulcher and departed.

61. And there was Mary Magdalene and the other Mary, sitting over against the sepulcher.

Meditation:

The body of Jesus Christ is put in the tomb by Joseph of Arimathea. The tomb is his own and he gives it freely for the rite of burial. The women have followed so that they can come after the Sabbath and prepare the body with spices and linens as was the custom of the times. There was every expectation of a burial. The Journey of the Christ was complete and the promise of redemption was sealed by his blood but the faithful knew not the hour or the form that salvation would come. What they knew was that they had loved Jesus Christ and that they would bury him in the tomb with love and devotion. What mysteries lay ahead they knew not. Jesus had spoken of his mission of having been sent by God to bring about the redemption of mankind and they believed in that redemption.

You have taken the path that Jesus took to the cross and beyond. You have stood where he stood and in a small measure felt what he felt that on that terrible last walk. Your devotion will carry you forward to salvation if you will but be faithful.

Your meditation:

_____
_____
_____
_____
_____
_____
_____
_____
_____
_____
_____
_____
_____

Station XIV

The Scriptural Way of the Cross

A Modern Change in the Way

In 1991, his Holiness Pope John Paul II introduced a new devotional Way of the Cross. The traditional version, which had been established for over 600 years, had five stations which had a traditional basis not a scriptural basis and his Holiness wanted to provide a devotion which would be more closely designed to Scripture replacing those stations without a scriptural connection. It should be understood that both are valid for meditation and devotion. Both help us to understand the last journey of Christ and both let us journey with him and share the last walk which he took to redeem us.

These stations were set up at the coliseum in Rome and set up on Good Friday, 1991. He celebrated that form leading the procession until he was no longer physically able to do it. After that a stage was set up so that Pope John Paul could watch the procession.

In 2007, Pope Benedict XVI gave his blessing to the form of the Way and thereafter both forms of the last Journey of Jesus are approved. For the pilgrim, both are the most moving devotions in the church and help us to understand and share in the Suffering of our Lord as he suffered to redeem us. All Christians can benefit from this devotion.

Let us begin.

Station I   **Jesus in the Garden of Gethsemane**

We adore You, O Lord Jesus Christ, and we bless you.

Because by Your holy Cross, You have redeemed the world.

Matthew 26:36-39

36. Then cometh Jesus with them unto a place called Gethsemane sit ye here while I go pray yonder.

37. And he took with him Peter and the sons of Zebedee, and began to be sorrowful and very heavy.

38. Then he saith unto them, My soul is exceeding sorrowful, even unto death, tarry ye here, and watch with me.

39. And he went a little further, and fell on his face, saying, O My Father, if it be possible, let this cup pass from me; never the less not as I will but as thou wilt.

St. Luke 22:43

And there appeared before him an Angel from Heaven, Strengthening him.

Meditation:

Jesus knows that this very night he will be taken and tomorrow he will be judged and punished by crucifixion and he has sought the solitude of the Garden of Gethsemane to pray. He brings his disciples with him and asks Peter to watch over him but his disciples fall asleep and Jesus in his reflection of that which he must suffer fears in his heart. He asks his Father to take the burden off of him but he knows that the prophecy must be fulfilled. We can share this feeling with Jesus. We often encounter things in our lives which we must face and yet we fear those things. We too wish that they would pass from us. God sends an angel to Jesus to strengthen his resolve because the redemption of the faithful hangs in the balance. This final chapter must be completed.

Your meditation:

_____
_____
_____
_____
_____
_____
_____
_____
_____
_____
_____
_____
_____

Station One

Station II   Jesus is Betrayed by Judas and Arrested

We adore You, O Jesus Christ, and we bless you.

Because of Your holy Cross, You have redeemed the world.

Matthew 26:47-48.

47. And while he yet spake, lo, Judas, one of the twelve, came, and with him a great multitude with swords and staves from the Chief Priests and Elders of the people.

48. Now he that betrayed him gave them a sign, saying whomsoever I shall kiss, that same is he: hold him fast.

And forthwith he came to Jesus and said Hail, Master; and kissed him.

John 18:2.

And Judas also, which betrayed him, knew the place, for Jesus ofttimes resorted thither with his disciples.

Meditation:

Jesus who had come to the Garden of Gethsemane often to pray is now on this final night betrayed by one of his own disciples. Judas Iscariot has brought the Temple Guards to arrest Jesus and to be sure they arrest the Savior he has told them he will give them a sign of a kiss to Jesus so that they will know him. We understand betrayal. We can suffer this betrayal of our Lord because we too have felt betrayed at times. Often it is those that we hold close to us that do it. Jesus has no anger in his heart for Judas for he is simply fulfilling the prophecy and he is the chosen one to betray his master. Jesus has only forgiveness for Judas. Jesus is here to redeem us and that can only be achieved by the blood of the Savior. Judas is but a part of that prophecy and must complete his portion of it. Suffer this betrayal with our Lord but let his example of forgiveness be in our hearts as well.

Your meditation:

_____
_____
_____
_____
_____
_____
_____
_____
_____
_____
_____
_____
_____
_____
_____

Station Two

Station III   Jesus is Condemned to Death

We adore you , O Lord Jesus Christ and we bless you.

Because by your Holy Cross, You have redeemed the world.

Matthew 27: 1-2

1. When the morning was come, all the chief priests and elders of the people took counsel against Jesus to put him to death.

2. And when they had bound him, they led him away and delivered him to Pontius Pilate the Governor.

Matthew 27: 20-2*3*

20. But the chief priests and elders persuaded the multitude that they should ask for Barabbas and destroy Jesus.

21. The Governor answered and said unto them, Whether the twain will ye that I release unto you?

22. Pilate saith unto them, What shall I do then with Jesus which is called the Christ? They all say unto him, Let him be Crucified.

23. And the Governor said, Why, What evil hath he done? But they cried out the more, saying, let him be crucified.

Meditation:

Consider that Jesus has now been arrested, bound and accused of blasphemy, the priests and elders here have brought Jesus to Pontius Pilate, the Roman Governor of Judea, because only he has the power to condemn Jesus to death. Pilate finds no fault with Jesus under Roman Law but the priests and elders demand that he be crucified. Pilate gives them a choice in front of the gathered crowd to either free a criminal named Barabbas or to free Jesus of Nazareth but they incite the crowd to say free Barabbas and Pilate orders Jesus to be beaten and washing his hands of it, Jesus is taken to be crucified.

Your meditation:

_____

_____

_____

_____

_____

_____

_____

_____

_____

_____

Station Three

Station IV   **Jesus is Denied by Peter**

We adore you, O Lord Jesus Christ, and we bless you.

Because by Your holy Cross, You have redeemed the world.

John 18:17, 25-26.

17. **Then saith the damsel that kept the door unto Peter, Art thou also one of this man's disciples? He, saith, I am not.**

25. **And Peter stood and warmed himself. They said therefore unto him, art thou also one of his disciples" he denied it and said. I am not.**

26. **One of the servants of the high priest, being his kinsman whose ear Peter had cut off, saith, did I not see thee in the Garden with him?**

Peter then denied again and immediately the cock crowed.

Meditation:

Peter had told Jesus of his undying love in the Garden and said that he would always be with him. Peter was the disciple who pulled a sword and cut the ear off of the Guard which Jesus had healed for the Guard. Jesus had told Peter that Peter would deny Jesus three times that very night before the cock crowed.

Jesus has now been taken and the disciples are sorely afraid that they too will be taken and fear has over-taken them. How alone Jesus must be. How we seek to deny our Lord in the face of ridicule and the fear of being taken and punished. The disciples loved Jesus and they believed in him but they knew not what was going to befall him and were afraid for themselves. Imagine what we would do if we feared for our very lives and all we had to do to avoid that which we are afraid of is to deny that we are Christian and a member of the faithful. Jesus knew what was coming. He knew the cup that his Father had set before him. The disciples did not. In his fear Peter denied his master and it was painful for him to do that. We should reflect and share in our love of Jesus and not deny him now.

Your meditation:

_____

_____

_____

_____

_____

_____

_____

_____

_____

_____

_____

_____

_____

Station Four

Station V   Jesus is Condemned by Pilate

We adore you , O Lord Jesus Christ and we bless you.

Because by your Holy Cross, You have redeemed the world.

Matthew 27: 1-2

1. When the morning was come, all the chief priests and elders of the people took counsel against Jesus to put him to death.

2. And when they had bound him, they led him away and delivered him to Pontius Pilate the Governor.

Matthew 27: 20-23

20. But the chief priests and elders persuaded the multitude that they should ask for Barabbas and destroy Jesus.

21. The Governor answered and said unto them, Whether the twain will ye that I release unto you?

22. Pilate saith unto them, What shall I do then with Jesus which is called the Christ? They all say unto him, Let him be Crucified.

23. And the Governor said, Why, What evil hath he done? But they cried out the more, saying, let him be crucified.

Meditation:

Consider that Jesus has now been arrested, bound and accused of blasphemy and the priests and elders here have brought Jesus to Pontius Pilate, the Roman Governor of Judea, because only he has the power to condemn Jesus to death. Pilate finds no fault with Jesus under Roman Law but the priests and elders demand that he be crucified. Pilate gives them a choice in front of the gathered crowd to either free a criminal named Barabbas or to free Jesus of Nazareth but they incite the crowd to say free Barabbas and Pilate orders Jesus to be beaten and washing his hands of it, Jesus is taken to be crucified.

Your meditation:

_____
_____
_____
_____
_____
_____
_____
_____
_____
_____
_____

Station Five

Station VI   Jesus is Scourged and Crowned with Thorns

We adore you O Lord Jesus Christ, and we bless you.

Because by your holy Cross, you have redeemed the world.

John 19:1-2

1.   Then Pilate took Jesus, and scourged him.

2.   And soldiers platted a crown of thorns and put it on his head.

Mark 15:17

And they clothed him in purple and platted a crown of thorns and put it on his head.

Matthew 27:26

Then he released Barabbas unto them, and when he had scourged Jesus,
he delivered him to be crucified.

Matthew 27:29

And when they had platted a crown of thorns, they put it on his head and a reed in his right hand and they bowed the knee before him and mocked him, saying Hail, King of the Jews.

Meditation:

Jesus beaten and mocked, bearing the crown of thorns, is led away through the crowd. The crown is painful and humiliating, Jesus bears this for our sake and our redemption and we contemplate his suffering as our own. We understand his pain and understand that, while he is innocent, we are not and he pays this price for us. He pays this dreadful price because we cannot. It is through his suffering and God's grace that we will gain the Kingdom of God not through our efforts but through his sacrifice.

Your meditation:

_____
_____
_____
_____
_____
_____
_____
_____
_____
_____
_____
_____

Station Six

Station VII   **Jesus is Given His Cross**

We adore You O Lord Jesus Christ, and we bless you.

Because of Your Holy Cross, You have redeemed the world.

John 19:16-17

16. They delivered him therefore unto them to be crucified. And they took Jesus and led him away.

17. And he bearing his cross went forth into a place called the place of the skull, which is called in the Hebrew, Golgotha.

Meditation:

At that time only Romans could conduct an execution and in the practice of crucifixion, the accused would carry their own cross to the place of death. This was the burden that Jesus had to carry. While this was done as a punishment, Jesus did it out of promise and eternal love. It was part of the redemption of man that he carry this burden and while suffering the beating and crown of thorns and the humiliation that he had undergone that day this physical burden he also had to endure. His burden was so great yet his promise so much greater still for in that promise lay the everlasting life of the faithful. This cross he did bear for all mankind. We can but reflect in wonder at his sacrifice.

Your meditation:

_____

_____

_____

_____

_____

_____

_____

_____

_____

_____

_____

_____

_____

_____

_____

_____

_____

_____

_____

_____

_____

Station Seven

Station VIII Simon of Cyrene Carries the Cross

We adore you O Lord Jesus Christ, and we bless you.

Because by your Holy Cross, You have redeemed the world.

Matthew 27:32

And as they came out, they found a man named Simon by name and they compelled him to carry the cross.

Mark 15:21

And they compel one Simon, a Cyrenian, who passed by , coming out of the country, the father of Alexander and Rufus to bear his cross.

Luke 23:26

And as they led him away, they lay hold upon one Simon, a Cyrenian, coming out of the country, and on him they laid the cross, that he might bear it after Jesus.

Meditation:

It was Passover and all Jerusalem was filled with Israelites from far and wide, come to celebrate the Passover. They had come to worship and bring their sacrifices to the temple. They came from all over Judea and while many had heard of the promised of Jesus many had not seen or heard him speak the word of God.

There is no indication from scripture that Simon was a follower of Jesus Christ only that he was selected from the multitude for the holiest of duties. He helped Christ in a way that any Christian would have been moved to do. He eased the burden of the cross from our Savior's shoulders. He eased the pain of the Cross from digging into the flesh of our Lord. Which of us would not give up our lives to have been that person? Here at this station we can meditate on how we would serve to lighten the load of Jesus and how we can serve others as he has served us.

Jesus often taught of the importance of how we treat each other. In fact it is central to his teachings that we love each other as we love God. He had preached that we must relieve suffering and serve each other. That whosoever would be the last will be first.

Your meditation:

_____
_____
_____
_____
_____
_____
_____
_____
_____
_____

Station Eight

Station IX   Jesus Meets the Daughters of Jerusalem

We adore You, O Lord Jesus Christ, and we bless you.

Because by Your Holy Cross, You have redeemed the world.

Luke 23:27-29

27. And there followed a great company of people, and of women, which also bewailed and lamented him.

28. But Jesus turning unto them said, "Daughters of Jerusalem, weep not for me, but weep for yourselves, and for your children.

29. For Behold the days are coming, in which they shall say, blessed are the barren and the wombs that never bare"

Meditation:

Jesus continues to struggle with the cross and out of the gathered crowd of people who are reviling him comes righteous women who are weeping for him. They seek to comfort him but Jesus tells them of a tribulation coming for those who do not follow the Lord their God. Generations yet unborn will bear the sins of this day and living a righteous life will reward them. He wants them to understand that a price will be paid for those that are not the faithful. We should feel the burden he has undertaken to save us and bring everlasting life to us but also to understand that everlasting life is not without a price, He pays the price for us and all we have to do is follow him and follow God's Law. Those who will not will pay a price hard to bear and suffer because of it. His sacrifice has sealed the promise but we still must understand that sacrifice and live our lives as if it is a sacrifice that we shared.

Your meditation:

_____

_____

_____

_____

_____

_____

_____

_____

_____

_____

_____

_____

_____

_____

_____

_____

_____

_____

Station Nine

Station X   **Jesus is Nailed to the Cross**

We adore You, O Lord Jesus Christ, and we bless you.

Because by Your Holy Cross, You have redeemed the world.

Luke 23:33

And when they came to the place which is called Calvary, there they crucified him, and the malefactors, one on the right hand and the other on the left.

Mark 15:25-28

25.   And it was the third hour and they crucified him.

26.   And the superscription of his accusation was written over, THE KING OF THE JEWS.

277. And with him they crucify two thieves, the one on his right hand and the other on his left.

28.   And the scripture was fulfilled, which saith, and he was numbered with the transgressors.

Meditation:

As we reach this spot the full knowledge of our journey is upon us. We have seen our savior suffer and be reviled and we bear witness to all that we have seen. We bring with us our devotion to his sacrifice and our devotion to his relieving us of our sins. We bring a sense of the pain that he suffered and we have shared in that pain with him. We wait now for the inevitable outcome and we watch as the crowd mocks him and can do nothing but stand silent because this is the fulfillment of the prophesy. His disciples are in the crowd but their fear makes them silent. They have been hiding in the crowd for the whole journey. He has made this way of sorrows alone but now we have walked with him. We bring our own fears and sorrows with us to share in his pain and with that we share in the redemption he has promised and that promise has been sealed with his blood.

Your meditation:

_____
_____
_____
_____
_____
_____
_____
_____
_____
_____
_____
_____
_____
_____

Station Ten

Station XI Jesus Promises His Kingdom to the Repentant Thief

We adore You O Lord Jesus Christ, and we bless you

Because by your holy Cross, you have redeemed the world.

Luke 23:39-43

39. And one of the malefactors which were hanged railed on him, saying, If thou be Christ save thyself and us.

40. But the other answering rebuked him Saying, Dost not thou fear God, seeing thou art in the same condemnation?

41. And we indeed justly; for we receive the due reward of our deeds, but this man hath done nothing amiss.

42. And he said to Jesus, Lord, remember me when thou comest into thy Kingdom.

43. And Jesus said unto him, Verily I say unto thee, Today shalt thou be with me in paradise.

Meditation:

Here we have the promise of our redemption. Two criminals crucified with Jesus, one who asks if he is really the Christ then save them all showing doubt and at the same time asking to be saved from the earthly punishment. The other simply believing in Jesus asks for nothing. He realizes the innocence of Jesus and understands that while he deserves his punishment Jesus is being punished for all of us. Because of his faith in Jesus his salvation is promised and Jesus responds to the man that "Today you will be with me in paradise." not because the man deserves it by deeds but because his faith in Jesus is strong. This is the promise that Jesus gives to all of us. This is the promise of the sacrifice of Jesus.

Your meditation:

_____
_____
_____
_____
_____
_____
_____
_____
_____
_____
_____
_____
_____
_____
_____
_____

Station Eleven

Station XII   Jesus Entrusts Mary and John to Each Other

We Adore You O Lord, Jesus Christ, and we bless you.

Because by your holy Cross, You have redeemed the world.

John 19:26-27

26. Now there stood by the cross of Jesus his Mother and his mother's sister, Mary the wife of Cleophas and Mary Magdalene.

When Jesus therefore saw his mother and the disciple standing by, whom he loved, he saith unto his mother, Woman, behold thy son!

27. Then he saith unto the disciple, Behold thy mother! And from that hour that disciple took her into his own home.

Meditation:

Jesus seeing his mother standing by the cross with one of his disciples John whom he loved, and he entrusted them into each other's hands and from that day forth they took care of each other. Are we not called to take care of each other in the same manner? Jesus knowing that the end is near and his task is almost complete gives this final duty to his mother and to John that they care for and look out for each other. We, as we stand at this station, contemplate both the salvation that Jesus gave to us and the pain of his mother as she watched his final hours. We have walked along with Jesus and we are not alone. He is with us always and that is his promise but he calls us to do for each other also. He by his entrusting of his mother to John and John to his mother serves as the example of how those who follow him are required to take care of each other.

Your meditation:

Station Twelve

Station XIII   Jesus Dies on the Cross

We adore You, O Lord Jesus Christ, and we bless You.

Because by Your Holy Cross, You have redeemed the world.

Eloi, Eloi, Lama sabachthani?

Mark 16:34

At the ninth hour Jesus Cried with a loud voice, saying, Eloi, Eloi, lama sabachthani? Which has been interpreted, My God my God why has thou forsaken me?

John 19:30

When Jesus, therefore had received the vinegar he said it is finished and he bowed his head, and gave up the ghost.

Luke 23:46-47

46. **And when Jesus had cried with a loud voice, he said, Father, into thy hands I commend my spirit: and having said thus he gave up the ghost.**

47. **Now when the centurion saw what was done, he glorified God, saying Certainly this was a righteous man.**

Meditation:

Jesus cries out from the Cross and darkness covers Jerusalem as his spirit passes. The Temple Veil is torn and silence spreads out over the multitude. Even the Roman soldiers fear for what they have done. In his final hours Jesus has given forgiveness to his persecutors. He has cried out to God in pain and suffering, seeking God's help. Let this terrible last journey be over. Each of us can feel the suffering and pain and now that the end is here we can praise God that it is finished. Jesus is beyond the reach of mankind and those who have hurt him and made him the object of so much scorn and pain. Jesus said as his spirit passed "It is Finished."

What do we, the faithful, do to atone for mankind's part in this. How do we exhibit the devotion to show we understand and have suffered with Jesus as we walk this last journey with him? Jesus died in this most terrible way for our salvation. He died for our eternal life. He died to give the faithful a room in his Father's house and he has gone on to prepare it for us.

Your meditation:

_____

_____

_____

_____

_____

_____

_____

_____

Station Thirteen

Station XIV   Jesus is Laid in the Tomb

We adore You, O Lord Jesus Christ, and we bless you.

Because by your Holy Cross, You have redeemed the world.

Mark 15:46-47

46. And he laid him in a sepulcher which was hewn out of a rock and rolled a stone unto the door of it.

47. And Mary Magdalene and Mary the mother of Jesus beheld where he was laid.

Matthew 28:60-61

60. And laid it in his own new tomb which he had hewn out of rock and he rolled a great stone to the door of the sepulcher and departed.

61. And there was Mary Magdalene and the other Mary, sitting over against the sepulcher.

Meditation:

We understand now that the people who so lovingly took the body of Jesus Christ down from the terrible Cross knew nothing of what was to occur in the following days. Their love was based on his teachings and the promise of salvation that he gave them. They revered him for who he was and who they believed him to be. Now we know the Kingdom of God and that is what they could only have had faith in. They believed what he had foretold but knew not how it would come about. We see clearly while they could only see dimly and theirs is an example of the faith that we all should have in order to gain the Kingdom of God.

Joseph risked much to claim the body of Jesus by going to Pilate. It could not be hidden from those who had mocked Jesus and asked for his execution but he went ahead and did it anyway. His body needed to be prepared in the manner of the custom and his followers who had been so afraid before now came forward to do what had to be done to prepare Jesus for burial.

The body of Jesus Christ is put in the tomb by Joseph of Arimathea. The tomb is his own and he gives it freely for the rite of burial. The women have followed so that they can come after the Sabbath and prepare the body with spices and linens as was the custom of the times. There was every expectation of a burial. The Journey of the Christ was complete and the promise of redemption was sealed by his blood but the faithful knew not the hour or the form that salvation would come. What they knew was that they had loved Jesus Christ and that they would bury him in the tomb with love and devotion. What mysteries lay ahead they knew not. Jesus had spoken of his mission of having been sent by God to bring about the redemption of mankind and they believed in that redemption.

You have taken the path that Jesus took to the cross and beyond. You have stood where he stood and in a small measure felt what he felt that on that terrible last walk. Your devotion will carry you forward to salvation if you will but be faithful.

_____

_____

_____

Station Fourteen

Addendum

We have now walked and suffered with Jesus Christ through his last hours. The Way of Sorrows as originally blessed by the Franciscans or as re-affirmed by Pope John Paul has been your pilgrimage. You have walked in inspiration as Jesus walked and have meditated on his suffering and the giving up of his earthly being.

Modern usage has brought about a call for a Fifteenth Station and many churches have added that to the Way. It represents the final stage and the ascendancy of Christ to his Father's house. There can be no redemption without the suffering of Christ because his sacrifice is what brings us that redemption. Many believe that the Stations as a sublime devotion should conclude not with the suffering but with the glory of a risen Christ. That is his promise to us. We conclude this devotional with a Fifteenth Station. We, unlike the disciples and followers now know of the ascension of Christ and the promise that the faithful will follow.

Station XV   **The Ascension of Jesus Christ**

We adore You, O Lord, and bless you.

Because of Your holy Cross, You have redeemed the world.

St. John 20:11-17

11. But Mary stood without at thee sepulcher weeping and as she wept she stooped down and look into the sepulcher,

12. And seeth two angels in white sitting, the one at the head and the other at the feet, where the body of Jesus had lain.

13. And they say unto her Woman why weepest thou? She saith unto them, Because they have taken away my Lord and I know not where they have laid him.

14. And when she had thus said, she turned herself back and saw Jesus standing but she knew not that it was Jesus.

15. Jesus saith unto her, Woman why weepest thou? Whom seekest thou? She supposing him to be the gardener saith unto him, Sir, if thou have borne him hence, tell me where thou hast laid and I will take him away.

16. Jesus saith unto her, Mary, She turned herself and saith unto him, Rabboni, which is to say, Master.

17. Jesus saith unto to her, Touch me not; for I am not yet ascended to my Father; but go to my brethren and say unto them, I ascend unto my Father; and to my God, and to your God.

_____

_____

_____

_____

_____

Station Fifteen

About the Author

D.L.Grant

D.L.Grant (Dan) spent many years as a Deacon and Elder and a member of the governing body of his church. He trained through the Bethel Bible Education program and taught Adult Christian Education at his church in addition to religious education to children from 3rd grade through high school. He was inspired to be baptized into the Christian Faith as an adult at the age of 25. He was baptized along with his wife and two children.

D.L. served as a member of the board of directors and is now president of, Changing Images Art Foundation, a nonprofit organization whose mission is to provide "**Medicine for the Soul**." Changing Images brings child appropriate art to children in pediatric wards and institutional settings changing the visual setting of children, some of whom will never live outside an institution. Changing Images has been working with volunteer organizations to provide artwork in hospitals and special needs schools around the world since 1997. They also work with older adults in nursing homes, shelters and rehabilitation institutions including VA hospitals.

D. L. Grant was inspired to write this layman's guide to the **Stations of the Cross** through his studies and devotions to the Scriptures and to help increase the understanding of the message and promise that comes to us through the life, death and Resurrection **of Jesus Christ.**

About the Illustrator

Arlene RB Sullivan

Arlene is an art teacher at Morris Catholic High School in New Jersey as well as the Executive Director/Artist and co-founder of Changing Images Art Foundation, Inc. She has been recognized with many awards for her continuing efforts in providing "**Medicine for the Soul**", on a worldwide basis.

- 2008 Nominee/Finalist 1010WINS Community Service Award

- 2008 Jefferson Awards Honoree & Medalist recipient

- Nominated Extraordinary Volunteer VMC 2006

- Nominated/ finalist **Russ Berrie Make A Difference Award** 2004

- Nominated **Woman's Day Magazine Award** 2003

- Invited to be one of the featured authors for Dr. Seuss Day, Read Across America at the TH Rogers School in Houston, Texas. Also visited the Esperanza School 2/2004

- NJ State Legislative resolution Honoree for Changing Images – 2002

- Wrote and illustrated The Journey of Hanna Heart , a children's book inspired by the murals she paints with children in pediatric units.

Sullivan was inspired to illustrate this book through her love of art and teaching. It is her hope that this book will encourage students of all ages to more fully understand the message of love and promise that is offered through this journey.